The Wind Southerly

The Wind
Southerly

Heather Ross Miller

Harcourt, Brace & World, Inc., New York

Some of the poems in this book originally appeared in *Coraddi, Impetus,
The Phoenix, The* Raleigh *News & Observer, The Red Clay Reader,
Reflections,* and *Southern Poetry Review.*

All these poems are for *Melissa*

and also for the memory of *Randall Jarrell*

CONTENTS

The Wind Southerly

A RUSH OF WINGS

In the beginning
    There was one man and things he loved:
Wild rose and thyme,
    Lemons growing in tubs,
    A greenness,
    A rush of wings he loved.

Ivy grew through the walls. Through the very walls. *Imagine!*
The ivy curling there, so quietly, taking apart the shingles
And the nails,
Re-appearing, unnoticed for weeks,
Toward the throat of the chimney.

Then there was Janah.
Her hair hung so straight down her back,
So straight, so black, so goddamned down—
You wondered what held up that mess of hair.
Janah had a mole on her arm.
    One brown petitpoint mole,
    On the underside of her arm,
    Inward,
Toward the breast.
Like the rest of her,
It was enchanting,
Enchanting because it marred,
    Would not be washed away,
    Would not be moved.

Thyme and roses,
Lemons, almond-buds, lime.

3

They flutter in the darkness.
    A rush of wings settles over the place
    Where ivy pushes through the wall—
Where ivy pushes,
And the girl pushes,
And the man, unmolded,
    Lets them.

SNOW PRISON

In the places of wide snow wind,
Earth and sky curl an infinite blue nail.
The holly rustles autumn-awkward
Over an iceburned broken trail.
An old bird in the tree, young snowbirds on the crust—
How many times will their voices rust
And scratch the pane of winter?
The window of winter is a tight tear-freeze
That numbs over.
You look through this window of winter—
Empty sill, no tarts to steal,
The round breath of children peels
Across the pane in flakes.

Deer dints in the morning, and bird feet,
And strange prints always small and skippy
Through the snow.
What if there was a big moon last night
That made you hear brooms and tinkle-ice
In the pine webs?
Oh, brush it up this morning,
In the ice litter, with the shivery bird chatter,
And throw it out the door.

QUEEN ANNE STREET

The Chinese children clatter above me on wooden sandals,
Pounding, leather-bound,
Small pointed feet of pigs.
Across Queen Anne,
The cathedral chimes
Whatever iron hour it is,
Whatever iron hour it was,
Whatever iron hour it shall be.

A shelf of settling snow.
The window is a shelf of settling snow,
White-flecked and powdered,
As soft as the shawl on my son's bed.
It was there when he fell asleep
And it will be there when he wakes.
And when he wakes and looks at the snow,
How shall I go lightly into his room
And lift him up to the sound of dead wooden feet?

After lunch, the snow melts to grey stone.
And an even greyer sky sheds its outgrown skin,
Split, white and dry, to the bone.
My son wakes, crying alone.
In this grey city,
One small crying thing is not heard,
One small cry is snowily blurred.

GILEAD

You come from a long house,
A long stone house of prayers.
River Sundays and muddy barefoot praise
Damned up the days of your summer riot.

I don't know that house.
My house was a windmill,
Moss-stacked and tall,
A dim green glimmer in the heat.

We look in the book of your house:
The men and their women peel brownly,
And their legends stiffly crack.
You say:
> "Grandpa went round on Sunday mornings
> To every house;
> Knocked on its door with his big blue knife,
> And collected his nigger rent."

Your Grandpa wore several white beards,
Not one, but several,
Rippling across his old face like frosty vines.
And your Grandma held a German silver purse,
A grey crushed mesh of vanity.
The cradle, church, and churn had left famine,
Flood, no fire.
She was more buttonhook than woman.

Grandma and Grandpa rose to their river church on
    their river Sunday

In the green rush of a river-strangled May.
There the hollow wives sat beside their strange mates,
And the twining ivy starved with God.

When they returned,
Stiff and hot in the new spring balm of Gilead,
He was calm.
He picked up the poker
And struck her, the wife of his bosom.
Severely, methodically, without passion,
The black soot streaked her pale old-fashion skin.
She put up her hands,
Like poor old ivory fans
Left over from a masquerade.

Then he left her by the best hearth,
Swept bare of fire,
In the stiff front room where a tall mantel clock
Ticked stupidly;
And the frozen stares of her children
Stared frozenly out their heavy oak frames.
He went to his barn,
To his rope that he had thrown up over the loft beams
In the cool, fluttering, early morning.
"There is a tree in Gilead
That shall heal the sin-sick soul."
The field lark sang.
The horses frisked;
Their big veins twitched with the blood-push.
He stood,
Still calm.
Oh, balm of Gilead,

Sweet mint of my father,
Caress me.

You have said these gifts are mine:
The big blue knife, the stiff buttonhook,
Grey German silver, sweet balm of Gilead.
But I say I don't know that house.
In the still early morning,
Let us flee.
Let us take the balm and steep it into sweet tea.
The book of my house is full of blank pages.
No green river riot rages
In the cool clover-white of my house.

When their Sunday is over,
And the muddy feet have stamped out the mounds of
    their praise,
We can walk on to higher grounds in warmer days,
Through the rank wild green,
Easy, quiet, faintly incarnadine.

APION

I

Tscharner stood in the door.
"You might not leave me again," she said.
One hand gathered the bedclothes,
One small nail-pink hand.
"I might be dead."

"Might," he said and shut the door.
Ravens screamed over in the deer pine.
He made his slave gather boughs
So that she might have light
And, also, warmth.

Tscharner rode down Apion,
His black cape striding the wind.
He forded the rushing streams and resisted the ravens'
   screams.
Back there, the woman ignored his hard-gold ember
And threw open her curtain,
Letting in the poison-cold December.

II

A gangrenous leg turned black. The old woman puts
   mold on it.
White bread, the flesh is black.
I am bread, I am black, I am turned to mold.

Tonight he rides like the scourge of Egypt,
His cape black, his eyes black. His lancet is very sharp.

Doctor Tscharner, my love,
My sharp cold love.

Kaethe, listening in the night, heard voices.
It was the sound of the Falls,
The drowning, rounding sound roaring and pouring
Through her chambered ear.
She combed out her hair. The voices hissed like fire,
Then went out. Beyond Apion, long past the Falls,
Came a new voice,
The voice of Tscharner's hoofbeats, pelting sternly
    through the frost.
Sharp as flint, the voice came, clear.
Kaethe ceased to hear.

THE MARSH KING'S DAUGHTER

The nightcool air fingers my curtain.
The sound of wind across bird backs
Feathers me,
While the dark cocoon of sleep begins to spin.
Ponds and pools,
Rivers and runnels
Ripple the round warm caves of my sleep.
Along the shore
A white canoe pauses;
The golden slipper-fish plunge deep.

I am alone in a water canyon.
I rise a little in this lonely sea,
But a quilt of marsh elder subdues me.

My little dress is of white linen,
With blue silk stitching upon the hem;
My poor little dress,
White and thin and dim.
My sandals are buckled with marsh grass,
Long green thongs,
Spangled in the sheenwing of dragonflies,
Studded in the brilliants of peacock eyes.

As I sleep,
My hair floats out in a wild luminous corona.
I am a daffodil, a jonquil, a milkweed;
I am a total eclipse,
A ruddy yellow ellipse.

My lover must walk on stilts
Or fly with wings of wax to reach me.
But the marsh would eat his stilts
And the sun would drink the wax.

His voice runs in and out with sea,
Drifts in and out with my breath.
It is a soft death
To sleep this way:
The feel of the sea night and day,
The tones of his call to rise, fall.

Perhaps, I could tie my little dress
Into a white sail,
A small thin sail
To propel me across the marsh.
But if I reached the harder land,
There could be no anchor.
I would be a strange water child,
A woman from a far country.

So I shall sleep here
In the warm cocoon of marsh grass.
When the storks come in spring,
Their sharp cries will shake
This sleep from me.
My little dress will wither away,
The blue silks will shred;
My new body will step gently
Over the thin white dead.

THE COMET

Thrusting west,
Bright hairs combed out in a tail,
The comet appeared, just visible,
Over the beam of the barn.
It had no business
Flicking so nervously in the dark
And scattering fiery hairs all over our yard.
And neither had you any business sitting there
So primly in the black grass,
Your sharp bright face
Sighted westward,
Up skyward,
Watching that comet usurp the sky.

Strangers appear.
They get themselves born in country beds
And are christened.
Comets, without warning, seize the sky
Late a country evening,
While potatoes still bubble in the pot.
And late a country evening,
You watch the fiery sky,
Biding time, biding time.

OCTOBER 1965
For the memory of Randall Jarrell

There is no more of that which filled us.
In doorways, unthinking,
From windows, our arms sunk to the sills,
We have been murmuring.
In thin new voices we have been murmuring,
　　Come home, little friend.

How we sigh. It is too sunny. The wind southerly.
How we turn from the view.
How we pick up and go on, go on, new and unlovely, unclean.
We do not mean it. We do not mean.

Within warm rooms, walled with brick and cinder,
To a thickness, perhaps, of six inches,
He read to us.
　　Gerontion,
　　　Inversnaid,
　　　　Coos.
The bus changed on Spring Garden.
We sat,
In plaid and khaki capes,
White napes bent over the word,
Cigarettes tilted.
The world lilted. It trembled and it sank.
We sat. So comfortably we sat and didn't thank.
We did not mean it then,
And now we shall never mean it.

Off Florida tonight the October hurricane turns.
The seas gather themselves and churn at the bottom of the
    world.
Lord of all gentleness,
Send out the bombers, the bears.
This emptiness wears on us
And we cannot put it off.
It says to us:
        Be good. Fold your hands and learn the lesson.
        Confession. Learn to come down.
But this lesson has no sound.
No sound of highroad, the dry leaves crackling,
All locked up,
                swollen shut,
                            buried.

Rivers flow off from us,
Tumbling down to the sea.
The ball-turret gunner has sunk, face down, in his womb.
Here, by the mock-orange tree,
Here is well water.
We are washing ourselves with well water.
We will be clean again.
        Come home, little friend

ENCOUNTER

It was last night.
Moonscent and wildscent lay upon the air;
The stiff pine hair
Stirred uneasily.
And I stepped from my stone to moss.

The deer lifted.
Flinty feet,
Black quiver-wet noses,
The ancient flickering eyes of beasts waiting in the wood:
Dimly they stood
In ancient gazing poses.

The fragrance of suspicion
Passed between us
Like a watercloud before the sun.

The old doe snorted.
The others, obeying,
Fled.

What old evil out of the long dark of life
Had fallen there?
Upon us in the wood?
That once warm play of brown sunlit fur,
That limber laughter of thin bare flesh,
A boy and fawn . . . ?
The green gaywings have flown.

Now I hunt alone,
In a dark forest,
In a month of winds,
To the noise of dogs.

QUAIL WALK

Every afternoon at four,
The quail pass our door in quietness.
Black-crested,
Soft, and neat,
They put their feet down to earth
In care,
Prudently attentive to fear and anger there.

The open road blankly bares.
They pause;
Then break,
One after one after one,
And none dare to look.

If a brother lies broken,
Brown feathers in a sack,
The spaniels circling;
What use is it?

Home, home to the brushy nest,
In a line exact and discreet,
Black-crested,
Soft, and neat.

GUNNERY

We found notes the ammunition girls had smuggled:
 My name is Wanda Sue Ketchum.
 36-21-36. Buena Vista.
What kind of babe would put her name in this?
Wanda Sue? Sounds southern. No, Oklahoma.
The aroma of smoking guns
Enwombs the sea.
The target sleeve descends,
Swollen, unbleached belly of muslin,
Strafed in seven colors of paint.
It hovers for a moment like a gull,
Then sinks into the sea unquestioningly.

Over the beaches the children scattered,
Their fingers purple and naked.
At night we waited, wearing goggles to replace our eyes.
Outside the sea slipped past the bow—
Shining, slipping sea—
And the catapult, like a monster's slingshot, took hold
Of us and flung us far.

Deep inside a voice, a young one, kept saying
Beyond me, beyond me,
Like a barb of gold, the sun!

Wanda Sue Ketchum went to work wearing bright curls.
In drab olive she sat, her fair lip pursed.
She sat packing shells and bullets, mortars, torpedoes,
 shrapnel.

We were torn apart.
The pieces floated toward the beaches,
And beyond the beach was the sun.

WAIANAE MARY

In Waianae,
On the island of Oahu,
Was Mary the big Hawaiian,
Six feet tall and fullblooded,
Fat and interminably pregnant.

She worked in the sugar refinery
Until the ships had brought her boys:
    A shack in the cane so full
    The sides seemed to breathe.

Her naked babies ran about harmless and uncensurable.
They got hungry,
So she punctured a can. The heavy milk flowed from its
    arrows,
The arrowhead nipples of the Carnation can.
Their milk was warm. They sucked and swarmed.

The ships at Pearl
Let loose other children, also hungry,
Full of impurities,
Mary's boys.
They followed like chicks, like pups,
Buried and contained by her,
Transplanted through the surf that shook the beach.
"Sailors, U.S.," she growled, then,
Scratching her bulbous nose,
Grinned.
Boys and babies, naked babies, naked boys,

Refined and evaporated, reduced to their purest state,
Wallowed her in bed, kissed, thrilled;
Six weeks, maybe, following,
Themselves delivered on deck,
Were strafed and killed.

THREE COWRIES

Over Oahu, the palms flutter and bang
To green shutters against a broken wall.
A surge of white attacks the beach,
And retreats,
Swiftly bleeding in translucent blue.

I reach.
I attack you,
But I cannot bleed.
You stand there holding three cowries
You found beneath the reef,
Brown-flecked,
Firm-leopard, precisely closed as a leaf.

MIDWATCH

I have stood by.
The sea sleeps clean.
Earphones buzz and hiss, but say nothing to me.
And I say nothing to the fo'c'sle.
We are as silent as the sleeping sea.

When, approaching harbor, they sound the fathoms,
They find at ten, a red rag,
At fifty, a rope with three knots,
And at one thousand, the chain comes over the side,
Brightly dripping,
Bearing nothing but its own wet links.

I have stood by four hours from midnight.
The sea sleeps clean and empty,
Delivered from her first-born son.
I remove the earphones, still warm,
And go to my billet, where,
Spinning into a hammock,
I sleep,
Brightly delivered,
Bearing nothing.

GRANDMAMA LEDA

After church on Passion Sunday,
She took them by the hands.
Pale curls had slipped and strayed guileless under ear.
"Come, dearies, I'll show you Hell."
Their Sunday dresses lily-belled
And their Sunday lockets gleamed a dull heart's-ease.
She marched them down the red rut road.
It was April and new calves bleated by the fence.
"That preacher's got no sense. Tub of gut! Hell ain't fire.
It's this!"

Up walnut stairs,
The satin balustrade poled their palms,
Knotty-calloused and rose-petaled.
The little girls flocked like covey on her hem.
She opened the door and drew them in.
"Stand here."
Down the bombazine curtain, blacking out the light,
Shut to the door and lock up clickering cluck-tight.
"Dearies, here's Hell."

All black.
And on the far south wall, framed in glass,
One big swan hoists his big snow wing.
The little girls stand waiting,
Red-sprigged, lily-belled, locketed in gold,
They wait for the stab,
The hot swift rush to enfold.

But instead,
Grandmama opens the door and lights break through bom-
  bazine.
"Now you seen," she crackled, "don't forget!"

Don't forget.
Blackness and a swan
Who raises his white wing.
Downstairs, under the smell of onions,
The dining cloth patched and one spoon dented,
The little girls walk out.
They throw cracked wheat to the geese in the yard.

One on each side of the fire, we sit.
Long ago I rocked the children and put them in their bed.
Outside, the night horses pass,
Striking sparks against the road.
You rise and dim the lamps of tin and glass.
The horses pass.
Their hooves fade into flickering flames upon the ceiling.
I rise to brush back the cinders
And stumble on my long white gown.
And you,
You are strongly there,
Fingers flexed under my arm, cheek red from the flame.
Then we sit again,
One on each side of the fire.
And I look at you and marvel.
How many years you've existed without me.
In just five seasons of my time,
A wedding, two children, a fireside in the night.
How many nights before me you sat beside a fire,
Drowsy on your mother's neck,
Then later, a boy.
So many nights,
So many fires,
The horses clatter and red-furled ashes fall to the hearth,
Die.

DECLINE

In the high October woods,
There is a quiet spot
Where not one hand disturbs the air,
And dew remains unbroken on the grass.
A lone grey fox can pass about the magic rim,
His narrow eye first bright,
Then again dim.

It is the place for an old woman,
On a quiet evening,
On the last one left,
To come and sit and tend her fire,
Like the others,
The young ones,
Tend their cradles.

Next morning,
Those embers shiver into ash
And sift away like snow.
The passing fox pauses to sniff the air,
Then seeks his burrow.
And winter comes,
Certain as death,
Like an old woman with one hand on her hip
And a great shortness of breath.

POEM FOR MY DAUGHTER

In the pale April rain,
I walk the deer park.
Silently, on buckhorn and clovernubs,
Honeysuckle, maypop, sage, and scotchbroom,
Silently, the thin rain rubs.

In the cool echo of rain doves,
I remember my name,
My name in summer, at evening.
There the boo never murmurs.
And his hot wild honey
Is figged, peared, appled,
Syrup and sunjell dappled.
Here the wet wild bee
Flutters and falls.

The birds lay blue eggs, I know.
And the birds' blue shells
Were part of that simple blue
Seen in a wide-washed sky and infant eye.
And the warm palm-clouds swung their fronds
Before the royal marching sun.
Still the clouds swing:
      They turn and face east for one half,
      Then, turn, and face west for another.

You only know rock pools
Where red fish glimmer cold.
And little girls bend to fret the ripples
Under a freckled sun.

You are sweetly with me,
Here in the deer park,
In the rain-pale, green-dark evening.
The red fish feint away,
And you blame it on some Jack-with-a-lantern elf.

Rain doves call wearily.
And my summer name settles wornly
Among the damp pale trees,
Too nervously stirred by a night-spiced breeze.

AWAKENING

When I wakened,
I had not locked the last night's door.
Open it stood upon a day not let in;
A simple woodsman's sill
Framing wilderness unwelcome.

A honeysuckle vapor hung over my path,
Wreathing and curling,
Gathering into a tall white genii,
A deadly genii disinherited by the sudden sun.

Shall I arise to chant old carols?
Go out and cross this path,
Then cross it again?
Strip mistletoe from high branches?
And slit my young lamb's throat?
Such charms are sure to some,
To heal a deed undone.

A child is born upon a rose petal.
The rose swells into a willow.
The tree bursts open white wings
And flies away a swan,
A swan bearing this young child upon its wing.
The woman whose child this is,
Does not recall the rose.
She strips the willow for baskets;
She strangles the young swan.

TWO WINTERS AND ONE SUMMER
FOR MY BOY

It has been two winters and one summer
Since his sign flashed upon the autumn sky.
He stands before me,
Pure and unsullied,
A spikelet of grain.
Back then, in that summer not his,
When he slept beneath my skin,
Due south;
Back then I did not know my boy.
Now I see his eye, still blue,
Dark hair soft along his cheek.

Tonight above south coast,
The handle of the Dipper bent and spilled out
Silver flecks of grain.
Two winters and one summer
Stand behind my boy
The Dipper cannot fill up again.

KASSANDRA

Here upon the even of this night,
I am with oaks. The heavy sun flows dripping
Through oak-green veins.
A tide goes out in the sky like a flock of hungry birds.

My father's grain leans upon the night, heavy-sweet, russet:
All the vintage of my father's hand,
And I his tender grape.

In the shrinking forest,
Leaves and fern shed dust. The tattered air turns red.
A deer lingering makes coronet of yellow horned head.

My father's vines are not yet spoiled,
But the white pod of the ironweed blooms upon the highway.
There will be frost soon. And the moon is full of tears.

The sun has coiled its honey beneath the ridge.
Some few sweet strands fleck out, then die.
Like the silent deer vanishing with no trail,
The night descends on a raven-swift sail.

My father's young children that dance with pale hair,
All these children are shaken from him
Like petals in the frail rain.
And I remain,
His rose, his little queen,
To spin and weep and tell the tale again.

Ah, Ashenputel,
Little rose, little queen.
The fair fine hair falls down;
The tears drop into cinders,
And the cinders drop into dust.

HANSEL

Little sister, in this night
Do not falter.

I have heard them in the next room speak.
And the sound was the sound of one last bough
Laid on the fire to burn.

For the witch is not old,
But young and lovely,
And dainty of foot.

Sister, do not give way. See! Behind me the pebbles fall,
Left, and now right,
Like milk, like snow
In the dew of night.

SHE BEARS

I

My miserable child cries now,
   against me
   in the miserable young day of my beauty.

She cries.
And my round heart thumping soundless in soundless flesh
   makes no reply.

O daughter—to have sons is to have sons.
To bring forth girl-children in this sick warm season
   is to bear scorpions.

II

And in the sick warm season,
Wet mushrooms rip the cancerous earth,
It is then the bears come out of slumber
And tread through the forest.

Up from Bethel, on the outskirts of the world,
The children gather to mock the old men with bald heads.
The bears come forth and tear them into little pieces.
And the children do never know
That the old men they mock
   are but themselves;
And the bears that devour them are mothers.

A DELIRIUM

The copperas waters of Council Springs,
Glassy, virulent, gold-spilled rings,
Keened dull tongues and pickled the limbs.
In the huts above the spa,
Old women, stoppered in glass,
Their vinegar turned to blood with rage,
Watched to see what came to pass.

We came. The buggy bulged with haste.
Derry dropped his chicken in the dirt
And Mama pinched his ear and scolded "waste!"
The others asked,
"Poddy, is this where the Indgens come?"
"Yes," replied Poddy, "they come and held their parley."

Council Springs,
Basketed by trees and convoluted rock-mossed hills,
Fed from secret veins,
Blood-sour, the sting of vinegar,
Warbled over toes and flushed away the pains
Of old men, old women, paralytics, melancholy brains.
Coppery water spurted in the sun like an opened artery,
Then sped downhill.
All the ill it bore within its breast
Surged to fever-crest.

After picnic, after melon, lemonade,
I stole away to wade.
The copperas waters of Council Springs,

Glassy, virulent, cold-gold rings,
Rose and reared and shook my knees,
Chillblend, pitchblende, deep down, darkened.
"Poddy, did the Indgens really?"
"Course. To parley."
They squat on the bank to watch,
Unstoppered, red.

"Derry, Derry. Git to the buggy. Git!"
The children shadow-faded through the trees.
I stood in the dust with glistening knees,
In the stammering, stupid dust.
Council Springs, bright as rain, plunged through me,
Leaving a dull spit-brown stain.

DECEMBER 1941   LITTLE BROTHER

When Willie May came in the morning,
She stooped to poke the fire and said,
  "I had me a dream,
  And he ain't dead."

The flames she had roused,
Bristled up to argue,
Then died back down to drowse and whine in the grate.

I sat and tapped my plate and waited for Willie May to say
How she knew.
But she went out to boil our clothes,
To beat the foam across the board,
And wring and squeeze and peg
Our pot of garments on the wind.
She washed everything and hung it out to dry.
Even white folks' sin.

The orange coach came and drove us away
To the stout stable-bricked school.
We read and wrote and counted all a winter's day.
And those lessons passed like scrolls unspiraled
Through a glass:
  Tigris and Euphrates,
  Perpetual Persian Gulf,
  The abacus bead,
  The Egyptian reed,
  Fold your hands. The hands are rough.

December homely dark along the pane
Of the bustling pumpkin coach,
Flaking its flamingo with ice.
And my brother somewhere in the bursting sea,
My soul-brother on the deck of his blistered ship,
My brother-soul charred,
Iced and flaked in crimson snow.

Willie May, you come to cleanse my shirt and bleach us
Out white. You talk of dreams
In a splintery, kerosene-lanterned, tar-papered night.
Bleach out my brother,
Clean, blooming. Bleach and boil. Raze out the rot.

But my lesson sternly reads:
    Hawaii, formerly Sandwich Islands,
    North Central Pacific,
    Annexed 1898,
    Abundant with palm, pineapple, and myrtle,
    A territory 1900,
    Now stoned, ripped, and plundered.

ABANDONED

To the east of Appalachia,
Lie the lands of his father.
They are many of pine garden,
Quiet sunbrowned deer,
And broad meadow.
The mill of his fathers has been sifted and sloughed away
Like the husks of grain and grass
In the sieve of a mid-June day.
The milldam is deaf with moss.
And the dusty miller is dust.
His rough Hollandish breeches flap and rend,
He is abandoned,
Winnowed,
Chaff in the hand of the wind.

The hand of the miller,
Once red and quick,
Has become yellow and blind.
His thumbs sleep in the millpond,
Dim slow quivers of the deep,
A spiny brown fish called the miller's-thumb.

The son of the miller,
The grandson,
The son of the fourth generation:
All are born.
They have slept in long low cradles,
Dark slender boats,
Rigged and railed in spindles and spools
Of the dark heartwood walnut.

The sound of the rockers
Became the sound of the scythe
Became the sound of the stone
Grinding and crushing the spinning seed.

The dark cradles have been burnt around a washpot.
Gowns of christening lace have folded into ash.
And the last son of the miller
Has gone to sea.

The miller's son has gone to sea,
Down to the sea in a ship of light.
Dews and showers,
Snows and hail and rain at night
Rise up from the earth,
Sustaining for a moment,
Then fall back.
They run in rivers to the great sea.

Black cradles, the christening, the flop of the windmill·
The flop of the windmill and the flop of the earth
Turning through blackest black.
The dress was stiff with urine,
Yellow dress, the baby's knees were raw.
He stood at the gate and bawled.
The flopping blades flopped on.

Now dark clouds shed,
Dark winds blow,
And grass springs, the waves run high on the beach.
The dove stirs, whimpering.

Leaves and columbine come forth
And the rushing rivers show yellow in the swollen sun.

But the burrstone revives not
And the wheel, watershot, lies on its axle.

BLACKOUT

Mama pegged out the night with clothespins,
Cheap wooden pincers grasping the linen
Like brave little crabs in the tide.

"Hush up," she would say,
"It will soon be over."

Long after she had rocked me,
I felt the arms tight around my arm.
I heard the dark heart beating upon my heart;
Mama's heart that beat on through evening
And the dark invading night.

Her little pegs bobbed against the full dim linen sea.
And the feverish candles she had placed on the mantel
Shivered fitfully.

By now the screaming thunder warriors
Fly upon my father.
They pierce his ship.
The redbauble-eyed fish dart and dive,
And the sea bubbles in his beauty.

In the dark I could see her hair,
Long and fair and full of light,
The young hair of a girl, not Mama.
Beautiful and cruel, with mountains and wild water,
She dreamed and clasped me to her.
I struggled and struck out with my hand

Releasing pigeons and doves,
Blossoming like some foolish tree
On a warm midwinter day.
I struck as a child.
Yet she rose and cupped me in her hair.

Almost like smoke above the broken harbor,
Morning rises with an opened palm.
My father's young bones glisten
And silent dolphins lead his ship into shadow.

I am the son, the sole surviving,
And I am tightly in bed,
Behind grey linen.
The minutes collect upon me like grains in a glass.
They build a reef on my soul.
Coraled,
Reefed,
I slumber fast,
And the red waves of my father break endlessly past.

LIZA MUMPFORD DREAMS

"We crossed the river in a bateau, you know,
Just a skiff.
The ribbons hung in my eyes and I was so scared
I wouldn't brush."

Liza Mumpford rocked.

"The river was swift then. Swifter, then, than today.
When we touched Southbank, it was a long way
From where we'd come."

She glanced at the clock.
It struck half-past.

"That was the last time I ever crossed in May,
With the water running and the wind like Babylon."

Tonight, behind the still rocker and vague clock,
Liza Mumpford woke and said to me at the foot of her bed,
"My son, I have dreamed a terrible dream!"
Then fell back dead.

PATH TO THE SEA

There is much to be said for paths.
For wild salt-grains riding
And wind shift-sands sliding the foot of the runner;
And the sound of the bosun's pipe
Hollowed over and over in the salty wrinkles of shell.
I have walked there
On the sea soil,
Full of the sea smell and the sea noise,
In my lovely long-legged leisure.
And I have seen the winking shells, wet and tumbled,
Pressed upon sand like holy, broken windows.
They have said:

> You are no longer a child.
> You are no longer.

The bosun's pipe, the shell, and the sea became
Amberhaze against the pane,
Browning acorns in a bowl,
A wild chevron of geese on the wind,
And my orphan hand on the door.

SALLY LOCKE

When I married Crawford in the preacher's parlor,
All my aunts said I had done well.
Then I went to keep his tall house
And to nurse his old mother.
She did not like my pie,
It was too sour, too sweet;
She would never eat anything I baked.
Soon my aunts began to shake their heads and said,
"Poor Sally."

I milked three cows a day,
Twice a day,
For near to thirty years.
Back then the hearths were open
And the fires always threatened to leap out.
I had to put my baby's dress under a bedpost
When I went out to milk.
He cried.
They all cried.
The old woman would say,
"Let him get burned and he'll learn."

When winter came I pieced quilts,
Hung from ceiling hooks,
The rough shreddings piled near my shoes.
All the short dim day and late into the sharp windy night,
I stitched the rags,
Making them follow a jigsaw fool,
Making them march across the needle into Log Cabin, Dutch
    Doll,

Evening Star, Sunflower, and Virginia Reel.
When my sons wed,
I gave them each a quilt and wrote their wives in my Bible.

Before long,
The wives came to nurse me in the tall fading house.
I was good to those girls.
I never fussed about their baking,
I never fussed about their making my chinaclosets
Into junkheaps.

When I died,
I left Crawford a clean worn house,
A pile of quilting scraps,
One pitiful full blown rose,
And several sons.

They have put me into a nice grave and built a fence.
Cedars sprout near by and the blackberries cling on briers.
Wild deer run in the wood. I ponder many things in my dust
And I would like to tell them to Crawford and his sons:
    The sun seems to rise and set
    In only a day;
    The smell of the pine, underneath,
    Is sweet;
    I want to go and kiss my dear young babe,
    But wolves howl in these woods
    At night.

A STORY AT BEDTIME

It was a short time ago—
    The years, the melted wax,
    How they run down and collect in the cracks
    Of a soul—
Get back to the story. Yes.
It was just a short time ago I saw
Foxfire. It was milking the creek in yellow curls.
It was alone in the dark.
Were you alone? Yes, alone. *In the dark?* Yes.
I was alone as little girls are alone.
And I saw, almost like last night this seems,
In a dream,
A little girl sleeping there.
All by herself? Yes, all by. *In the dark?* No less.
She was green as Circe. Green as the shade
At noon in July. *What's Circe?*
Circe is little girls alone.
Don't tell this story. Tell another.

About the ox who was made of straw?
All right. The ox was made of straw and pitch.
In the summer you planted pea vines. The black ox
Trod, trampling the vines. *I didn't plant pea vines.*
Yes, you did. The ox trod on them.
Tell about winter.
In winter the ox was cold. Icicles hung from his chin.
You brought him in by the fire and he melted.
A black pool of pitch by the hearth. And in the middle was a
    pea.

I am asleep. You are asleep.
Circe eats the ox. Foxfire burns. Circe eats the pea.
Trod on me, dead child,
Trod on me.